Stress free, Sorrow free and Peaceful Life

ER. BABAJI SAHOO

First published in 2020 by

Becomeshakespeare.com

One Point Six Technologies Pvt Ltd.

119-123, 1st Floor, Building J2, B - Wing, WadalaTruck Terminal, Wadala East, Mumbai, Maharashtra, India, 400022.T:+91 8080226699

Copyright © 2020 by

ISBN - 978-93-5438-037-2

DEDICATION

This book is dedicated to loving prime minister of India Mr. Narendra Modi as he is using principle of knowledge given in this book to administer India and own the heart of most people of not only India but the whole world.

He is on the job of alleviating poverty from India. This book will help him to make people of India and the world stress free, sorrow free and peaceful. The author is ready with a NEW INDIA project for the PM like "International Yoga Day" where people can get true and scientific knowledge, how to live happily and peacefully.

PREFACE

Welcome to your one stop solution towards sustainable stress-free life. Yes, easy to comprehend and easy to integrate actions into your life to yield the results of a happy, full-filling and peaceful life that you always wish for.

With the rise of globalization and consumerism culture, most of the people on this earth are suffering from stress. The spirituality has lost its role in contemporary life. No doubt, everybody wants peace in their life. But the mechanism to get peace is really a huge question.

After going through an enormous volume of literary works, biographies and autobiographies of eminent personalities, a step is being taken to develop a scientific strategy to adopt the peace in life. This rational and concise approach is unique and the knowledge in this format is not available anywhere in the world i.e. scientific knowledge on how to live happily, peacefully and stress-free in whatever profession and in whatever social strata one is.

The Knowledge covers all 5 aspects of life:

(i) Body (ii) Mind (iii) Relations (friends & family) (iv) Money (V) God

With this true scientific reasoning, one can live with wisdom, without subscribing to blind beliefs and unscientific religious practices and not falling prey to the so-called Gurus and fake Babas.

Youth, Students in Colleges & Universities and Professionals can benefit the most out of this knowledge.

Politicians can use this knowledge for a corruption free ethical society.

Read this simple explanation of the key five knowledge that eradicates sorrow and bestows a peaceful & happy life on you. This authentic solution is scientific, logical, easy to apply and is aimed at cutting through the layers mysticism to create a sorrow-free life.

CONTENTS

1. What Do You Want?

STRESS-FREE, SORROW-FREE >> PEACEFUL LIFE

What you want from whatever you are doing from childhood to death?

Answer is happiness and only happiness. To live in peace and be happy, is it not?

Not only that, no work i.e. eating, talking, walking, reading, etc. are not possible unless you are in peace. Hence peace is inherent in you. Not that objective of life is to get peace. In actual life, happiness comes and vanishes quickly, and sorrow prevails. So, what is to be done to have a stress-free peaceful life? Let us find an authentic solution as found after years of search and real practice.

2. WHAT PREVENTS HAPPINESS?

How to have a happy life is same as how to achieve stress-free, sorrow-free & peaceful life?

Stress and Tension is fear to achieve a target for which an activity is taken up. Stress and tension is born out of fear of not achieving a target for which an activity is taken up. Tackling the fear of failure means avoidance of sorrow, because failure and its fear gives sorrow. Hence all the problems of the life will be solved if sorrow is eradicated. Lord Buddha in sixth century B.C. gave eight sutras like right paradigm, right remembrance, right action, right living, right expression, right commitment, right effort and Samyak Samadhi. To understand and apply these sutras is very difficult and very little use now a days. Understanding and applying effective solution given here-in is sure to achieve desired results as it is simple, easy to understand and easy to integrate into one's life.

We will urge you to give full attention and sincerely apply this easy method in daily life.

WHERE DOES SORROW COMES FROM?

1. Family relationships – Relationship trouble between husband & wife and between various family members. Expectations, difference of opinion and lack of understanding leading to stress

2. Death in Family – Passing away of loved one

3. Business Failure – Failure in any activity taken, sometimes in-spite of right efforts

4. Fear of Examination – Students not achieving results as per their expectations

5. Interpersonal relationships – Workplace relationship stress between employee and boss, among co-workers

6. Ill health – Chronic health conditions

7. Lack of basic life amenities – not having access to ample food and shelter

Above are listed just few examples from the myriad life situations that generates sorrow for us.

IS IT POSSIBLE TO FREE FROM SORROW?

Whatever we are doing, we are doing it for our own happiness, but most of the time we are experiencing sorrow. Happiness is momentary. It comes and goes. Sorrow being experienced by all rich, poor and powerful; it seems it's not possible to free from it.

We solve all our problems only by proper scientific knowledge (Gyana). Hence it is certainly possible if one applies appropriate knowledge (gyana).

Then we must know

• What is Sorrow

• What Causes Sorrow

• How to eradicate Sorrow

3. WHAT IS SORROW?

Sorrow is different from pain. Our body is a wonderful machine having its own security system. Any imbalance that happens in the body which needs attention, we get pain so that we take care and get treated. Pain belongs to the body while sorrow is caused by mind and intelligence. Negative agitation of mind is sorrow while positive agitation is happiness. Intense sorrow leads to depression and suicide. Mind and intelligence are responsible for everything of a human being. So, in this context we must know what mind & intelligence are.

Volumes and volumes have been written about the mind, but in short, Mind is flow of thoughts as accumulated by the five senses and it is a subtle invisible material thing. Unorganized mind is like a monkey while organized mind is like a KaplaVrikhya (wish fulfilling tree). Mind is formed after a few months of birth and is influenced as per the situation one takes birth. It is highly changeable and plastic.

Mind is link between body and soul, between matter and spirit, moving from visible to invisible. It is between two opposites. Hence it is always in tense. It cannot be in ease. Mind is not a thing. It is a process. Process cannot be silent. It is moving from past to future. Hence always tense. It always wants to be occupied. If unoccupied then you will become conscious of inner process which will give you peculiar strange tension. Hence mind is bound to be always ill. It cannot be balanced as silence need.

Mind is created from without. When you are born you had just capacity to mind, but no mind. Just possibility. Society trains you capacity into an actuality. Hence Hindu mind, Muslim mind etc. Mind is orthodox as it is conditioned by past, society and others, for certain purposes. But life is always new. You are always in new situation. Hence there is always bound to be tension and conflict.

When mind ceases you are established in your witnessing self. In other states expect this there is identification and all identification constitute this world. If you are in identification you are in the world. If you are transcended, you are in bliss.

This world of bliss is here and now, right now. This very moment. Just become witness to the mind and you have entered.

All the techniques, all methods, all path of Yoga meditation are concerned with one problem, how to use the mind. Mind is with everyone. There is possibility of Light and darkness. Both are implied in it. Mind is neither enemy nor friend. It depends upon you, the soul who is hidden behind the mind.

You are in misery because for many lives you have used the mind wrongly. Mind has become the master. But it is nothing but an instrument, lust like hand feet, leg, etc. You have given too much power to mind. It will struggle hard if you put it in right place. What happen to mind if it is enlightened? It disappears as master and remains as a slave. Knowledge of this book will enlighten you.

MIND CONTROL

When we are working on a particular task of work, we need to have few thoughts only which are related to that particular task. Many times, these few thoughts are accompanied by thoughts of past actions or of future actions to be done or of other people and their words and actions. These thoughts are difficult to stop at times for many of us.

Specially students face this problems and loose concentration hence take more time to understand and remember the things. Such situation needed some positive thoughts like I am a pure soul having unlimited power and capacity. This will help in a negative situation too and pour thoughts an unnecessary nature reduces.

The best way concentrate is withdrawing the mind from the task for a moment and concentrate on the feet of your mother whom you love the most ask her blessing. Doing this several times during the task will make the mind silent. Remember true silence is few thoughts and positive and necessary ones with no negative and unnecessary thoughts.

Intelligence is also subtle and shows you fault of

others, creates inner restlessness, defends and rationalizes your own mistakes, creates arguments, keeps you engaged in worldly life, maintains you in duality of good and bad, profit and loss, etc. Be very careful that it also prevents you to take right step to be free from sorrow. text here.

WHAT CAUSES SORROW?

Our sorrow and happiness depend on desire fulfillment. Whatever you wish for, if it happens then you are happy or else you are sad. Hence, desire is the main cause of sorrow. But desire should be clearly understood. Life is not possible without desire. Desire is godly if it is for the well-being of all and not just an endless weave of self-fulfilling stories.

Desire is from mind and intelligence. Usual belief is that cause of happiness is money and power. Actually, no amount of money and power can eradicate sorrow. As you know Ambani brothers are richest persons in India, but still was fighting court cases over property. Jeffery Epstein a multi- milliner of USA suicide recently in USA jail. Similarly, chief minister of Arunachal, having immense power over the state, committed suicide.

HOW TO ERADICATE SORROW?

As mind and intelligence are causes of sorrow, then what is the medicine to the mind?

Medicine to the mind is knowledge (Gyana) and understanding. Hence only by knowledge, we can be free from sorrow. Knowledge and understanding are two different things. One can have knowledge without understanding, like one can know what earthquake is without understanding how it happens. You are teaching your little one addition '2 + 2' and say it is '4'. Your little one questions why it is not '6'. You explain with your four fingers. Now all their doubts are cleared. Hence, 'Understanding 'means, things are clear, and no doubts remain.

WHAT KNOWLEDGE (GYANA)?

This knowledge of life and its workings can be simplified to these five truths.
1.   Knowledge of Self. Who are you?
2. Understanding that World is governed by scientific circumstantial evidences (vyavasthita shakti)
3. Understanding the Law of Karma.
4.   Understanding and settling all FILES with equanimity.
5. Accumulate credit in the account of pure soul.

4. WHO ARE YOU?

When one is asked who you to a person are one replies that "I am Professor Dr. Pranav Mishra". Here "Pranav" is a name given by his parents to identify him as an individual. "Doctor" is a qualification which indicates that he done a PhD. in a subject, while "Professor" indicates that he is in a teaching profession. "Mishra" indicates his family lineage. Then who is he?

Also, if somebody is asked pointing one's head 'what is this?', one replies 'this is my head'. He says, 'My Head', that means he is not 'head'; then who is he?

When a child is born in hospital, one is given a tag immediately identifying male or female child along with mother's name. After some time, the parents give a name, according to which family one is born in, that is Hindu, Muslim or Christian i.e. Pranav, Ahmed or John. So, when a child takes birth, he/she is not born as a Hindu or Muslim or Christian. Then who is he/she?

The body is made of 5 great elements air, water, fire,

water and space (ether). So is mind. You might have seen some of your dear ones dying in your presence. Some people even die while working on the chair. The body parts are intact, but no movement and one is declared dead. What happens then? Some ENERGY has gone out from the body, after some time the body rots and smells.

This energy is called Atman, Consciousness, Self, Rooh, Soul and Spirit.

1. Atman is defined as that which is other than the five SHEATHS namely, a) Food sheath b) Vital lair sheath c) Mental sheath d) Intellectual sheath f) Bliss sheath

2. It is beyond three BODIES a) Gross (sthula)   b) Subtle (sukham)   c) Causal (karana)

3. It is witness of three states of awareness a) Waking b) Dream c) deep sleep

4. It is nature of a) Existence (SAT) b) Knowledge (CHIT) c) Bliss (ANANDA)

In this universe there are only two types of energy: Material energy and Spiritual energy. Spiritual energy is responsible for movement & growth, which indicates Life. Besides this energy whatever you see is Material energy. Life exists on this earth starting from bacteria, algae, amoeba, marine life to plants & trees to mammals & birds to Human beings, because all possess this spiritual energy. Hence this universe is just a play of energy (material and spiritual) i.e. cosmic (total) energy.

WHAT IS GOD?

As clarification is given about energy, it will be appropriate to discuss about God. This total energy or cosmic energy we may call God, Allah, Ishwar or the Supreme.

God, which is invisible, all pervading, all powerful, indestructible and unthinkable, is possible in only energy form. Just like radio waves and microwaves are present everywhere, similarly this cosmic energy pervades through everywhere in this universe. As anything in this universe is insentient material energy or sentient life energy, which is all part of cosmic energy. So, everything is God.

As to conceive cosmic energy is difficult it is better to concentrate on a Form (Rama, Krishna, Mohammad, Jesus, Guru Nanak etc.) you love most, and worship means surrender your ego. Best result you will get by worshiping your mother as GOD whom you love the most. Nature or GOD has made the law which is same for all. It is not that god will do special favors for you because you worship Him with full devotion. You can't become rich, powerful, cure your disease or pass examination doing nothing but just praying God. Law of karma will act God can't help you. Hence always do good karma, PUNYA.

To further clarify who you are, let us take an example. Electrical energy is present in different forms (body) like bulbs, heater, refrigerator, etc., which gives different effects like light, heating & cooling, etc. Similarly, spiritual energy is present in different life forms like plants, animals, male, female & children and they act differently. When electrical energy is taken away from appliances like bulbs etc., their functioning stops. Similarly, from life forms when spiritual energy leaves, it is declared dead. This clarifies that all life forms are part of God.

QUALITIES OF THE SPIRITUAL ENERGY (ATMAN/SOUL)

Original quality of soul is Peaceful, Powerful, Truth, Loving & full of Knowledge. Hence every human being always wants truth, peace & love – Sat-Chit-Ananda, by which God is also defined. This proves why, when a lie or untruth is told even to a habitual liar, he is furious. Everyone wants peace, even if they themselves act violently. All human beings want knowledge for all activities. Similarly, everyone wants to live in happiness. This proves evidently that quality of God is inherent in you hence you are part of God.

EGO:
Spiritual energy in the body is called as Atman/Soul. Atman identified with body & mind is called Ego. When you say I and mine, it is the Ego; Atman identified with the material body.

The entire existence with respect to an individual can be divided into two categories a) I or AHAM b) This or IDAM. Atman is the I(AHAM) and rest of the world is this (IDAM). But because of ignorance of my real nature I am identified with either the body, mind or intellect so I have false notion about myself. This false notion is EGO. If I can clearly distinguish what is different from myself, I can negate it and come to apprehend my own nature.

Ego is I thought. In its subtle form it remains a thought, where as a gross aspect it embraces the mind, the senses and the body. All of them disappear in the deep slumber along with the ego, similarly it will in death.

Ego is an entity independent of the self in order that it must be created or destroyed by itself. It functions as an instrument of self and periodically ceases to function that is to say; it appears and disappears. This might be Birth and Death. Relative knowledge pertains to mind and not self.

There is absolute self from which a spark proceeds as from fire. This spark is EGO. In case of an ignorant man it identifies itself with an object simultaneously with its rise. This association is ignorance whose destruction is our effort.

Actually, you are pure energy resting in the body. Due course of time, you are mistaken body and mind as you. Hence ego is born, a false I only for identification and exist in the society, different from actual I, the spiritual energy. Ego is responsible for all the activities, sorrow and happiness. Ego is the **doer, sufferer and enjoyer**.

But Ego is essential and protect you from your birth till adult hood, there after ego should be clearly understood and avoided else it will give you nothing but sorrow. Ego is cause of all negative qualities. Once only clearly understood it vanishes. Just think of tiny invisible germs CORONA-VIRUS can destroy the world and you are nothing significant. EGO gone you are the happiest person on the earth.

HOW THIS KNOWLEDGE OF 'SELF' HELPS:

This knowledge of "who are you" is a very important understanding, which will solve all your problems in life, and you will lead a peaceful life. With this knowledge you treat every plant, animal and human as pure Atman and part of God as you are. Practice treating your family members, parents, spouse, children, friends and neighbors as pure Atman as you are. Do not hurt anyone, mentally or physically. By practicing this knowledge all your accumulated negative energy will vanish. Treating all in equanimity will make you blissful and your family will be like heaven to live with.

Death means spiritual energy leaving one body for another. There is no death to you i.e. Soul or Atman. Hence thought of your death or your loved one's death will not give you any fear and sorrow.

5. WHAT IS THIS WORLD?

If you observe this world phenomena, everything is happening as per a scientifically logical law, like day & night for rotation of earth on its own orbit, like changing seasons for movement of earth on its orbit around the Sun. You plant a mango tree; it will not give a mango the next day. The tree grows with help of earth, air & water. It needs protection. It takes its own time to grow, flowers in time and then raw fruit comes out. Fruit grows & ripens in proper time, in a favorable weather condition. The pulp is eaten, and the seed is now ready for another tree. Hence things happen in right time and circumstances with support from various quarters.

YOU ARE NOT CAPABLE OF DOING ANYTHING ON YOUR OWN:

You are not capable of doing anything on your own, which you say proudly, "I did this or that…".

Let us take example of a tea making. You invited your friend for a cup of tea. And you are proud that your wife makes a very good cup of tea. For making tea, first water is required. How water comes to your house? It is lifted from underground or river, treated and supplied to you through pipelines. How much technology and people are involved? Similarly, fire, gas, electricity, sugar, milk, tea leaves, preparation kettle, serving pot, etc. are required which are prepared by huge factories involving thousands of people and agencies and finally reaches your house. You add ingredients with proper quantities and in time with good knowledge of tea making, then you say, "I made good tea". If it is overheated because of being unmindful, then what happened to the taste of the tea? Will you claim that you made the tea? You may say that your child cried, hence couldn't give attention or give some other reason. Hence circumstances are also responsible too. Many times, things do not happen as per your plan.

After making all efforts, whatever is the end result, is as per the scientific circumstantial evidences (vyavastitha shakti).

With this knowledge, your doer-ship claim vanishes. When you understand that you are not responsible for your failure in-spite of your best efforts, your sorrow disappears.

IS THERE ANY LIFE AFTER DEATH?

Before going to the law of Karma, the question comes is there any life after death. The question circles around if there are past lives, why we don't remember any of them.

Swami Vivekananda, the Indian scholar who gave the speech at the Parliament of World's Religions in 1893 in Chicago, denotes of our inability to recollect past lives to being thoroughly immersed in present experience creating a localized subconscious mapping. He likens that to while speaking a particular language, no words of other language comes to the subconscious, but as one tries to recollect another language, the words come rushing in.

You might have come across in media that a young person remembering their last parents, their last place of birth, etc. Recently on 25th October 2018, it was shown on TV news that twin brothers from Bagiyanath village of Sahajahanpur district of Uttar Pradesh, India, recognized parents and home of their last birth. On the Internet you can find many such cases. Art of Living in their 'eternal process', takes people through a six past lives vision.

Times of India, on 8th Oct. 2014 confirmed that 2060 patients in 15 hospitals in the USA, UK and Austria were taken for OBE (Out of Body Experience) and NDE (Near Death Experience). Out of 2060 patients, 330 survived after declared death with OBE and 140 with NDE. This shows that there is some continuation beyond the body.

Consider a desktop of computer. The computer is only, dealing with binary language and making all of its calculations in a language of millions of 0s and 1s. But for simplifying the access for the user, it converts it into a graphical form comprising of characters and images. The user doesn't comprehend the complexity lying behind. Similarly, Nature is cycling both 'genetic' data biologically and 'karmik' data spiritually. It then selectively allows the individual to access only relevant information required for the outer world survival to the subconscious. That doesn't mean that we are only what the present subconscious can comprehend of. These citations and several other cases point towards the continuous circle of life.

Let us consider scientific law, energy cannot be destroyed it changes form. When you drop a stone from a height the static energy changes to kinetic energy. Similarly, the spiritual energy present in every human body can not be destroyed. It moves on and enters in another body. Originally spiritual energy was pure, but it is contaminated when it leaves your body and move with mind, intelligence and sanskar. Be careful about your thought at the time of death. Your next birth will be in circumstances to fulfill your last desire. Hence revenge full thought will make you criminal in next life.

No thought no desire and no next birth. It is difficult but possible with continuous practice that is concentrating on cosmic energy GOD with out any desire.

6. LAW OF KARMA (ACTION)

Understanding the law of Action (karma), is very important to be free from sorrow. Before understanding law of action, we must know what action is. Action is performed in three steps:

- Thought – Before doing any action, first the thought arises. E.g. going to buy vegetables from the market. First thought arises that one should go and bring vegetables. Then, what to bring? What is required?
- Speech – One talks with family members. E.g. Then one discus with what to get or not.
- Actual Visible Action – Then the action is carried out. E.g. Then he visits the market and buys whatever is planned.

Thinking is a vital part of action, as it is the intention to act. Thought about act, even if you do not speak and act, is 'binding karma' and cause of 'karma effect'.

For example, a wealthy businessman donates fifty thousand rupees to a charity. His friend asks him, why he did so, and the businessman tells so that he wouldn't have donated a single rupee had it not been for the pressure from the mayor. Now what will be the fate of the act? The donation he made is a visible act, the reward for which he will get in this life when people praise him for the generosity. The consequence of intention (bhava) karma, "I wouldn't have given a single rupee", he will experience in his next life such a financial condition so that he will not be able give a single rupee. This is the subtle karma, which is the cause for his next life's circumstances. The donation made in this life was an effect of his good work in the previous life. One cannot understand something so subtle without knowledge (Gyana). On the other hand, when a poor man is asked to donate for a charity and his response is that he has only five rupees which he can give. He further earnestly feels that he would have donated five lakh rupees without any hesitation, if he had that kind of money. His donation of five rupees is the discharge of the karma created in his past life. But what does his present action yield in next life? He will be brought to such situation so that he is able to donate Five lakh rupees with ease as his effect of this Karma comes to fruition.

Many of us believe that God writes our destiny. We need to pause and introspect on this belief. If God wrote our destiny, two things would happen: First, since we are all children of God, all our destinies would have been equal. Second, as our parent, God would have written a perfect destiny for all of us. Today our destinies are neither equal, nor perfect. We also believe in the law of karma which states - As is my Karma, so will be my destiny. Our karmas are not always perfect, and we all do not create identical karmas. So, our destiny is neither perfect nor equal. We need to ask our self which of these two beliefs feels right for us. Karma means action. Law of Karma is about action and reaction, or cause and effect. Karmic law is constantly working in our lives as Karma includes our every thought, every word and every action. As per the Law of Karma, every action - however small or significant - has a consequence. The consequence is always fair. Right action brings a good consequence and wrong action brings a difficult one. Certain karmas may result in an immediate result. Other karmas may have consequence coming back an hour later, a year later, 20 years later, 50 years later, or in a future lifetime.

We can connect the karma with the consequence in some cases. However, when we see the effects of karma on a subtle level, we will not be able to connect consequence with the karma, since the karma might have been performed years ago or even in a past lifetime. So, we need not worry about that aspect of identifying the cause. It is enough if we remember that —

(1) The Law of Karma is always accurate and always fair to everyone.

(2) Our present situation is only a result of our past karma. So we are responsible for everything that happens to us.

(3) Our present karma decides our future so we have the power to create our destiny.

We have all experienced the consequences of both

right karmas and the wrong ones. Whether we believe in it or not, the Law of Karma is continuously in action. We need not fear the law but let us be aware of it. We also need to remember that Karma includes thoughts also, not just words and actions. So, let us focus on right thinking, speaking and behaving, so that we create a beautiful destiny.

There is a cause to everything happening to us. Happening is the effect of last life's karma. Cause-Effect is very scientific. As per science, to every cause there is an effect. Actually, what is happening to us, from birth to death is the effect of karma we have done in our last lives. This is called 'prarabdha' or accumulated karma and is discharged during this lifetime. Any new karma, we do in this will have effect in next life. We take birth in this physical body only to discharge karma, done in last life and desire at time of death.

TYPES OF KARMA
• Good karma (Punya) – Not hurting any Soul/Atman even in thought is considered as Punya, for which one will be rewarded in next life.
• Bad karma (Papa) – Hurting anybody even in thought will be Papa, for which one has to suffer in the next life.
Effect to good karma is happiness and effect to bad karma is sorrow. Good karma and bad karma don't cancel each other. Each individual karma must ripen to its respective fruition. In this life we have to discharge

the balance of karma done in so many lives. Law of karma is very subtle and difficult to understand; hence we must be careful. What time the karma effect will happen to you is also beyond our understanding. Even if to think and not speak and actually act, hurting, any atman is bad (papa) karma, for which the effect will result in suffering in next life.

NOBODY IS RESPONSIBLE FOR YOUR HAPPINESS OR SORROW

Sorrow or Happiness is of your own making. You are getting it because of your cause karma, only as an effect.

Everything happening to you is Justice as law of Karma is acting. When bad things are happening, remember this fact and do not react with negativity. Accept everything gracefully and remain calm. Thank God for the discharge of your bad karma and when all your karma good or bad is discharged, you will get free (mukti).

7. SETTLE THE FILES

Each 'File' is an Atman/Soul, related, known or yet to be known with you in this life. Father, mother, husband, wife, children are very sticky files. They are to be dealt very carefully. Anything good or bad you have done to any Atman, will meet you in this life either to give you happiness or sorrow to settle account of last life. Hence any Atman giving you sorrow, allow the Atman to settle the account calmly. Be calm and beg apology so that your previous bad karma is discharged. Do not react and hurt the Atman and consider him/her just as an instrument and do not create any further bad karma.

Bringing up children in a family specially for 1st time mother is always difficult task because she does not know who the child is and why he/she is born to her. The child is a soul and born to you either give you happiness or sorrow as per your relationship i.e. how much love and care you have given or trouble and pain given to him/her in past births. Hence you treat them as pure soul part of God Do not think you own them and control them as boss.

If they are violent and main cause of your sorrow be sure that you had treated very badly in the past life and they are here to settle the account. Hence treat them with utmost humility and beg pardon to the GOD for your bad karma.

Do not think a son is an investment to take care of you in old age or a daughter as cause of reducing your wealth and happiness. Each soul is here to exhaust his /her past karma and you are not responsible for their prosperity or suffering.

Hence become their friend and do what best you can, to live peacefully.

ACCUMULATE CREDIT FOR PURE SOUL

If you understand the above four facts, that means you have gained the true knowledge and will act sincerely in your life situations with the true knowledge. Then the fifth step will happen on its own. You will create good account for your pure soul.

IN SUMMARY

What you want is happiness and peace in life, remaining with your family and friends at the present national and global peaceful atmosphere, and pursuing whatever profession you are engaged in.

This is only possible in-case you apply the knowledge of these five truths sincerely in your family first and live with wisdom.

Right now, you are working all your life for your survival only. That is how to earn a living and have a comfortable life. Even after achieving it people compare with others. Without understanding the workings of life, the shallow comparison with others invites sorrow. You forget that you are mortal, and you will die sooner or later, leaving everything here.

All living beings starting from ants and animals survive in this world easily. For human it must be very easy. The sooner from a young age if one acquires this knowledge of the five truths and one applies, the more successful and peaceful one becomes.

Try to live applying this knowledge for a week only and experience what happens, as a trial case. This author and his friends are behind you to guide you in case you face any difficulties in application of this knowledge in actual life.

8. WHAT TO DO?

You have to do practically nothing special, not have to spend any money or extra time, take courses on 'how to be free from stress', visit ashrams of famous gurus, meditate and do yoga rigorously etc. If you apply this knowledge (gyana,) you will always be in a meditative state in whatever you are doing like studying, working as professional, doing business, etc. However, you have to practice the following as applying some of these gyana is very difficult in the beginning, because you are habituated to act differently in this and many past lives.

1. Good health and healthy lifestyle: As soul, spiritual energy has to stay with body till the prarabdha karma is exhausted we can attend happiness if the body and mind are kept in good health . For this proper exercise and food is a must.

Exercises
Every day in the morning or evening in empty

stomach the following exercises must be done for only fifteen minutes in even in your room or veranda. Sports-persons and who are doing regular exercises can do pranayama only.

a) Hand movement
b) Body movement
c) Jogging
d) Neck movement
e) Suryanamaskar (see Appendix)
f) Walking minimum 3km daily (for elderly people 50+ Years)

Pranayama
a) Vastrica pranayama
b) Kapalvati
c) Anulombilom
d) Bhamri
These pranayamas are taught by Baba Ramdev and available on the internet.

Food
To keep the body fit right type food is a must. Food should be testy and contain whatever the body needs.

As human being is not carnivore but more akin to a herbivore like a cow, our stomach is designed accordingly. We must take seasonal fruits (banana, guava, orange, ripe papaya, pineapple, jamun and other berries), green vegetables easily available in the market and milk along with carbohydrates like rice dal and roti. We must avoid oily and salty foods. Quantity of food must be 2/3 of what you feel full belly. Food should not be taken in hurry. Concentrate on chewing the food. Each bite must be chewed minimum 20 times. Water should be taken 1 hr. after the food unless there is emergency. Minimum three to four liters of water is to me taken daily as per season. Break fast, lunch and dinner must be taken at the time set by you daily at the same time. Timing is very important.

Sleep

Sleep is very important for good health. Try to get six to seven-hour sleep per day.10pm to 5 am sleep is ideal.

2. After getting up from bed and before going to sleep, say in a voice just audible to you, for one minute, "I am a pure and powerful soul". Powerful doesn't mean negative power driven by EGO but it means spiritual power which can i) Tolerate ii) Accommodate iii) Face up to iv) Pack up v) Discriminate vi) Judge and vii) Withdraw.

During the day, when you have free time, do the same as many times possible, while interacting with others, beware that they are originally pure souls.

3. Do not even think of any such thing that can hurt any soul. If any such thought comes to the mind, stop the thought and beg apology to God. Do not repeat the mistake. It will be difficult in the beginning but be assured that after some time it will become natural. Practice this first with your family i.e. parents, spouse and children.

4. Beware of your likes and dislikes. They force you to do good and bad karma. Like means Attachment (Raaga), while dislike means abhorrence (Dwesha). Just watch whatever is happening calmly. All fault is yours. Justice is happening to you all the time, as you are discharging karma of your past lives. Let the effect of karma take place. Do not create new cause karma. Be abitaragi (beyond likes & dislikes).

5. Beware of your ego. Any karma done with the understanding that you are not the doer but the instrument, things are happening as per scientific circumstantial evidence (Vyaavstitha Shakti), the karma will not be binding and no-cause karma will be done.

6. Get rid of anger and ego which effect peace and relationship in any sphere of life. It is also cause of ill health like blood pressure, heart attack, insomnia, back aches, digestive disorders .Ego is a weakness and instead of helping you to get respect loose respect. Anger do not help work done and efficiency as some people believe. Also, instead of anger helping you get love and co-operation from people, it makes you lose it.

It is a challenge to interact with people without being angry. Anger and ego are acquired sanskar but peace and love are every one's original sanskar.

When it comes to overcoming anger and ego,1st step is to look inwards and be aware that you are a peaceful soul. Influencing people is always easier that can take place with peace and love not trying to control them with anger.

Expecting or desiring a certain type of behavior from someone else, certain type of situation of your liking, is the root cause of all forms of anger. Avoid it.

7. Do not copy other people.

If some is not nice to us, we feel an impulse to strike back, tit for tat. Thus, we copy others wrong behaviors and give up our inherent goodness. When people are rude and disrespectful, we have three options

a. Reflect their behavior and deplete our virtues.

b. To absorb their behavior and go to pain.

c. To transform their energy radiating our inherent goodness.

We have power to be nice to everyone and not copy others behavior. Using my qualities consistently keeps me happy, contented and successful and earn blessings from others.

8. Being happy is the only way to give happiness.

The greatest gift we want to give is happiness. Despite providing physical comfort to our family and friends, they are unhappy at times. It is because we are unhappy. Being happy our self while discharging our responsibility, our happy vibration radiates and triggers the happy frequency in our loved ones and uplift their state of mind to happiness.

We have seen that despite extra effort to care, our family and friends are not happy with us. The truth is how much we do for people it does not matter. It matters how much happy we are while doing everything. It is your energy which influences others happiness. When you experience unconditional happiness, you have nothing but happiness to give others. In every sense contribute to-words creating a happy family, happy workplace and happy world by being happy always.

9. Do not resist change which is the main cause of stress.

Accept change. The inability to adapt to change is the most common reason for the life stresses that all of us are faced with. There used to be a time when change was not so sudden as it is now. The modern lifestyles have made change so sudden that we have reached a point where change resistance has almost become like a syndrome or illness.

10. Be stable in criticism.

Regardless of the form it takes and the intentions behind it, criticism can be difficult to accept. But if we learn how to deal with it, we can certainly benefit from the feedback. A large part of criticism directed towards us is not in our control, but how we respond to it is always our choice. No matter who you are or what you do, does someone always judge you? Even if things seem to be going well, do you find people criticizing your ideas, behaviors, talents, efforts or results? Like it or not, criticism is unavoidable, so it helps to take it in our stride. We need to be stable in the face of criticism. It usually comes with an energy of anger, insult, disrespect or rejection. So, more than the feedback itself, the accompanying vibrations hit us hard. Yet, we have the choice to only accept the feedback and be untouched by the negative vibrations accompanying it.

People's criticism is more about them than about us. It mirrors their weak state of mind – their hurt, their worries, their insecurities and their personalities. Basically, they are in pain and are relaying it to us. Our role is to understand, empathize and not radiate negative energy back to them. You have the power to make things better or worse when criticized. Be courteous to them, validate their words and improve yourself if needed. Otherwise release that scene from your mind. Remain stable in criticism, just as you remain stable in appreciation. Know yourself well and do not get disturbed when someone criticizes you.

Sometimes when sharing their feedback, people are rude, they criticize you. Pause and think through the criticism, check if it is valid. If yes, thank them and improve yourself. If not, let go, do not create any thoughts about what they say. Remain stable and don't react or argue or defend. Just state your views assertively. Understand they might be disturbed, jealous or insecure. Understand they are different, they are only expressing their opinion, which is based on their personality. Know your strengths and work on your weaknesses. Do not take criticism personally. Remain detached as you see their nature.

11. Be clear what are virtues and vices.
Peace, Power, Purity, Love, Bliss and Knowledge are Virtues which are your original qualities and qualities of the Spiritual energy that is the SOUL.

Always be virtuous.

Vices are

1.   Ego – Having no control over the Ego

2. Greed – acquiring material goods, more and more and more money and power.

3. Attachment – feeling of possessiveness.

4.   Lust – using excessive satisfaction through the senses as a means of fulfillment.

5. Anger – Fleeing of hatred and revenge.

6. Laziness – Becoming inactive on a spiritual, physical or mental level.

Avoid vices

Practice above with sincerity for a month or two and you will be free from sorrow and lead a peaceful stress-free life. You will be true Gyaani, enlighten or self-realized person. Free from sorrow is the first stage of MUKTI

In-case you can become bitaragi (beyond likes & dislikes) and act considering you and others as pure soul, part of god, karma will not bind you and you will be free from repetition of birth and death. This is second stage of mukti and is called liberation.

Please refer this book to everyone you know and request them to refer to everyone they know.

APPENDIX

SUN SALUTATION

ASANAS NAME (Positins Name)	ASANA (Position)
1. Pranamasanam Stand up strainght, keep your feet closed, bend your arms and fold your hands in front of your chest.	NORMAL BREATHING
2. Hasthaudhanasanam Raise your arms over head and bend back as far as possible; Keep your legs straight and relax your neck.	INHALE
3. Padhahasthasanam Bend down slowly; Palms should touch the floor completely; the tips of your finger and toech should build a line.	EXHALE
4. Aswachanach alanasanam Strech back your right leg; your right knee touches the ground and bring up your chin as far as your can.	INHALE
5. Parvathasanam Bring back your other leg; heels should touch the ground completely.	HOLD
6. Sastanganamaskar Lower your knees, chest chin and forehead to the ground; only your hips are lifted.	EXHALE

ASANAS NAME (Positins Name)	ASANA (Position)
7. Bhujangasanam Lower your hips and bend Lower your hips and bend back your upper body Keep your legs closed, chin up and look to the sky.	INHALE
8. Parvathasanam Your heels fully touch the ground.	HOLD
9. Aswachanchalanasanam Bend down slowly; Palms should touch the floor completely; the tips of your finger and toech should build a line.	HOLD
10. Padhahasathasanam Move your right leg to the front, bend down to the front, so that your chin touches the knee, Palms fully touch the ground and build a line with the toes.	EXHALE
11. Hasthaudhanasanam Raise your arms behind your head, bend back your upper body; try to see the inside off your palms.	INHALE
12. Pranamasanam Stand up straight, keep your feet closed, bend your arms and fold your nands in front of your chest.	NORMAL BREATHING

ABOUT THE AUTHOR

Er Babaji Charan Sahoo, born in the village Bari of Jajpur District of Odisha on 7th April 1945. Presently living in the steel city, Rourkela ,odisha, India.

A mechanical engineer from NITR (national institute of technology Rourkela), this is the first and only book of the author which he has written after years of spiritual research with practical association with leading spiritual organizations like ISKCON, ART OF LIVING, BRAHMAKUMARI, OSHO, DADABHAGAVAN, VIPASANA, etc.

Interacted with Maulanas of Muslim community and Fathers of Cristian community who consider this knowledge as one of a kind.

The only aspiration of the author is to impact the true and scientific knowledge to the world population so that they can lead a stress free, sorrow free and peaceful life without any blind beliefs and becoming pray to fake BABAS and GURUS. If the knowledge is applied with full understanding to your family members first, your family will be surely heaven to live with. The author appeal to the readers to sincerely apply the knowledge for only one month which will cost them nothing but may be some repeated failure of application of the knowledge to get out of negativity from his life. The test of the pudding is in its eating only. Fag end of life will be enjoyable only by hearing your story of happy and peaceful living.

The author can be contacted through Facebook, twitter and e-mail- sahoo.babaji@yahoo.com

9 789354 380372